Wasteland

Written and
photographed by

Colin S.Milkins

Artist: Roger Fereday

Wayland

STARTING ECOLOGY

Pond and Stream

Seashore

Wasteland

Wood

Editor: Sarah Doughty

First published in 1994
by Wayland (Publishers) Ltd
61 Western Road, Hove,
East Sussex, BN3 1JD, England

© Copyright 1994 Wayland (Publishers) Ltd

British Library Cataloguing in Publication Data
Milkins, Colin S.
Wasteland.– (Starting Ecology Series)
I. Title II. Series
574.5

ISBN 0 7502 0824 4

Typeset by Dorchester Typesetting Group Ltd, England
Printed and bound in Belgium by Casterman S.A.

What is ecology?

Ecology is the study of the way plants and animals live together in a habitat. A scientist who studies this is called an ecologist. An ecologist finds out about a habitat by observing the area and carrying out experiments. If you do the projects in this book, you will be an ecologist too.

Always go to wasteland areas as a group with a parent or teacher, and never wander off on your own.

CONTENTS

The words in **bold** are explained
in the glossary on page 30.

What is wasteland?

A disused railway line provides a home for wildlife.

Wasteland is an area of land that is no longer used. Sometimes it is an old railway line that has been closed, or land where houses have been knocked down. An area of wasteland does not have to be large. Sometimes it can be the edge of a car park or the corner of a school field that nobody uses.

Wasteland is never **barren** or empty. When an area is no longer used by people, it is soon taken over by plants and animals. Weeds, such as dandelions or coltsfoot are some of the first plants to begin growing in the area. After only a few months, seedlings of trees such as ash, silver birch and sycamore begin to appear.

▶ *A puddle may become a small pond for plants and animals.*

Soon birds, insects and other animals like foxes and hedgehogs come into the wasteland. They will be looking for food and somewhere safe to make a home. Small animals find homes in unusual places, such as broken walls, blocked-up gutters and even among old rubbish.

Perhaps you can think of a wasteland area near your home or school that you could safely study together with your class and teacher. Remember, some wasteland areas can be very dangerous, so never go there alone.

▶ *A house once stood on this area that has now become wasteland.*

Pathway plants

People sometimes walk through wasteland if it makes an easy route to get from one place to another. As they pass through, tall plants become trodden down and a clear path is formed. Dogs and foxes will also use the path and tread the plants down too.

If you look carefully at a path through the wasteland, you may see some plants that have not been damaged by people's footsteps. Daisies and **plantains** lie close to the ground, and their flat shape helps them to survive. If you trampled over daisies and plantains every day, they would still grow.

◀ *Tall plants grow either side of this wasteland path.*

You can carry out a study to see where daisies and plantains like to grow. Knock two short wooden poles into the soil at a distance of about 1 m from each side of a trodden path. Attach a string between the two poles. The string should be marked every 5 cm with coloured sticky tape.

▲ *A plantain is a flat plant. It is not damaged when it is trodden underfoot.*

Carefully follow the string from one side to the other. At each mark on the string look and see if there is a daisy or plantain on the ground. In your notebook make a record of your results to remind you where you found a daisy or plantain growing.

▼ *These children have set up the experiment to study flat plants on the pathway.*

Did your daisies and plantains grow among the taller plants or just on the path? Why do you think this is?

Sleeping daisies

▲ *This daisy has been cut in half. You can see the many tiny yellow flowers.*

▼ *Daisies at night, when the flower heads have closed.*

If you look carefully at a daisy, you will see the yellow flower head is made up of many hundreds of tiny flowers. Carefully pull a daisy flower head apart and find each little flower.

If you have a garden, find some daisy flowers on your lawn. Look at the flowers after it has been dark for several hours. You will see that the white petals have all closed up. They only open in the day. This is why they are called daisies or 'day's eyes'.

You can also study daisies during the day to see if the petals close in darkness. Find a good patch of flowering daisies on your wasteland or in the school field.

Put three black plastic flower pots over your patch of daisies so they are in darkness. Block up the drain holes of the pots so that no light can get in.

After half an hour lift one of the pots. Look carefully at the daisies and see if any of the flower's petals have closed, and if they have, make a note of this. After an hour lift another pot. Have the daisies closed? After an hour and a half, lift the last pot. How many daisies have closed? Make a note of your findings.

Using your results, can you say how long it takes for daisies to close after it has become dark at night?

▶ *The children are finding out how long it takes for daisies to close in the dark.*

▲ *Daisies on a sunny day, with the flower heads open.*

Litter

Wasteland has lots of litter on it. This is because no one looks after wasteland and clears it away. Most litter is dangerous and harmful to plants and animals, but sometimes good use is made of litter by the animals and plants that live in wasteland areas.

▲ *Sow some of your seeds on the bare soil, and about the same quantity underneath a crisp packet.*

▼ *This can of pet food has been thrown away and has filled with rainwater.*

If tin cans are thrown away, they may become filled with water when it rains. Soon the water in the tin can turns it into a 'pond' and it becomes a **habitat**. The water goes green as **microscopic** plants start to grow. Then mosquitoes and gnats lay their eggs in the water. Try making a tin can pond at home or at school. Leave it in the open and see what happens.

Crisp packets are very often dropped as litter. If a crisp packet gets stuck between some bricks or rocks on the ground, the soil underneath it becomes warmed. This has an effect on how well the plants grow. You can carry out a study to find out whether plants grow better if the soil is kept warm or cool.

Sow some wild flower seeds in a seed tray. Cover some of them with a crisp packet. After a week look to see what has happened. Have the seeds under the crisp packet grown better than the others? If so, do you think this is just because the soil was warmer?

Look underneath the crisp packet. Is it wet? If so, do you think the plastic covering has helped the plants in any other way?

This bath has become a pond for animals and plants.

Litter survey

Litter is not always useful to wildlife. It is often very harmful. Materials that take a long time to rot away are often dangerous for wildlife. Some animals like to crawl into empty milk bottles where it is warmer. They then cannot get out again and they starve to death.

This rook has caught a plastic ring around its head.

The plastic rings that hold drinks cans together can be dangerous too. Birds can get them caught around their necks causing them to choke.

You can carry out a litter survey on wasteland. The survey may tell you what type of litter takes a long time to rot away, and so is of most danger to wildlife.

First measure out 4 sq m of wasteland near the road or path where people walk. Collect all of the litter you have found in the square.

Sort your litter into the following groups. These groups are paper, glass, plastic and metal. Count each piece of litter in each group. Make a bar chart of your results. Now do exactly the same again, but this time measure out another square as far from the path or road as you can.

Make a bar chart of types of litter found in each area. Why do you think there might be more paper litter near the path or road? From your investigation, can you say what type of litter stays for a long time in the **environment**?

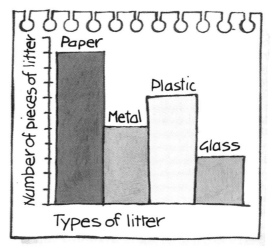

▲ A bar chart of a litter sample found near a road.

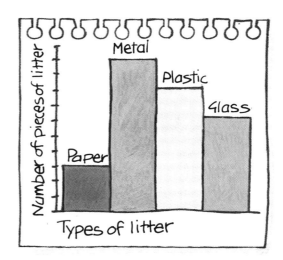

▲ A bar chart of a litter sample found away from a road.

Warning: Be careful of broken glass and jagged tin cans, they could cut your fingers.

The butterfly bush

▲ *A buddleia bush growing on the edge of a car park.*

▼ *A butterfly on a buddleia bush sucking nectar from the flowers.*

The butterfly bush is also called the buddleia. It is a bush that is often grown in gardens, but it is also very common on wasteland. Buddleia has lots of mauve coloured flowers that butterflies like to visit in summer.

The flowers grow at the end of the stem in large bunches. Each flower in the bunch is long and thin and is shaped like a small ice-cream cone. Only insects with long tongues can reach the sweet **nectar** at the bottom of the flower. Butterflies have long tongues and so they can do this.

Butterflies spend most of their day feeding. They fly from flower to flower until sunset when they settle down. The next day the sun warms up their wings and they start flying again. You can study the activities of butterflies. It is best to do this on a day when the sun keeps going in and out behind the clouds.

When the sun is shining, watch a buddleia bush very carefully. Count how many times you see any butterflies flying. Do this for 5 minutes. It does not matter if you count the same butterfly each time it flies. Then count the number of times you see a butterfly flying when the sun is in. Do this for 5 minutes as well. Record your results as a bar graph. Use your results to answer this question:

Do butterflies fly more when the sun is out?

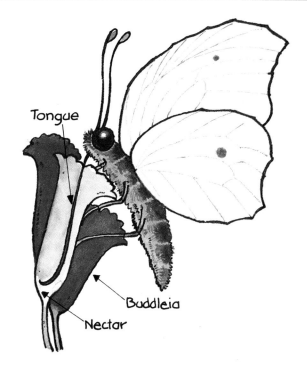

▲ *The long tongue of the butterfly can reach the nectar at the base of the buddleia flower.*

▲ *Draw a bar graph to show how many times butterflies fly.*

15

Poppies

Poppies in a farmer's field.

Poppies grow well on new waste ground. They also grow by roadside diggings and other places where the ground has been disturbed. Poppy plants can grow from seeds that have been buried deep in the soil for many years. Some poppy seeds can still grow after being buried for one hundred years.

To find out if poppies grow better on bare soil or grass you need to find a large seed tray for your experiment. Ask an adult to cut a piece of **turf**. Put this in one half of the tray. Put some soil or **potting compost** into the other half of the tray. Add some rocks or stones to the soil. This will make it more like ground that has been dug over.

Sow some poppy seeds on both sides of the tray. Leave the tray somewhere warm and in the light for up to six weeks. You will need to water the tray every day so that the soil and turf do not dry out. Soon the poppy seeds will start to grow.

Do the poppies grow better on your bare ground? Why do you think this is? What effect do you think the other plants in the turf have on the poppies?

▲ *Sow poppy seeds in the tray. The tray holds turf on one side and potting compost with stones on the other.*

▼ *Poppies grow on disturbed waste ground.*

The dandelion weed

▲ *Dandelions are weeds that grow well on wasteland.*

▼ *The fruits that make up a dandelion clock.*

Weeds are plants that grow and flower very quickly. They produce lots of seeds that are easily spread around. Weeds are able to grow in most types of soil. This is why new areas of wasteland are quickly taken over by weeds.

A weed that grows almost everywhere and is common in wasteland is the dandelion. The dandelion flower is like the daisy head. It is made of hundreds of small flowers. Pull a dandelion head apart and look at the flowers. Most of these little flowers will form a fruit with a seed inside it. You will see this as a dandelion clock. If you blow a dandelion clock you will see how easily the fruits are **dispersed**.

The root of the dandelion can make new plants if it is broken or cut into pieces. This could happen on waste ground if rocks and bricks were dumped there. The roots could also be broken if the ground was dug up by a digger.

Dig up the **tap root** of a big dandelion. Wash off the soil. Carefully cut the root into three or more pieces. Now put each piece into a container and cover with potting compost. Make sure the compost is moist but not wet. Cover the containers with cling film to keep the moisture in.

Look at the pots every few days. How many pieces of the root grow into new plants?

▶ *You can see the tap root on this dandelion plant.*

▲ *See how far the fruits are dispersed when you blow a dandelion clock.*

Snails

▲ *These snails are in their home. They have been marked by a blob of white paint on their shells.*

▼ *It can be fun to have a snail race.*

Snails are very common animals on wasteland. Look out for them hiding under stones during the day. At night they come out to look for food, especially if it has been raining.

If you find some snails in an area of wasteland, put a little blob of white paint on their shells. Also put a white blob on the ground next to them. Come back the next day and see if the snails have moved from their hiding place.

Find out where snails like to crawl. See if they prefer to crawl on rough or smooth surfaces. To do this, cut out a circle from a smooth piece of card. Now cut out some shapes from very rough sandpaper.

Stick these shapes on to a large piece of card. The pattern should be like a maze. Put some snails in the middle of the circle. They will come out of their shells and start crawling around. Look carefully at what the snails do when they bump into a piece of sandpaper:

Do the snails stop and change direction?

Do the snails crawl over the sandpaper?

Do you think snails mind crawling over rough things?

If you look carefully at the pathway of a snail, you may find that it leaves a trail of silver **mucus** behind. Try and decide how the mucus helps a snail to move across a rough surface.

The snail has avoided moving over the rough sandpaper.

Insects and flower colour

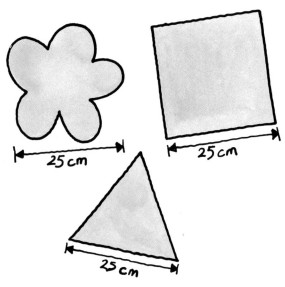

▲ *Cut out these three shapes from bright yellow card.*

▲ *Waiting for insects to land on the yellow shapes.*

Lots of flowers that grow on wasteland are the same colour. Buttercups, dandelions and coltsfoot are all yellow. Many insects visit these flowers. They will be searching for nectar in the flowers.

Find out if it is just the colour of the flower that attracts the insects, or if it could be the shape of the flower too. Cut out three large shapes using bright yellow card. One should look like a flower. Another should be a square and a the other a triangle.

Now lay the three shapes out on the ground near some flowers where insects are flying. A bright warm day is best for this experiment.

Be patient and watch the shapes for 10 minutes or even longer. Make a record of how many insects land on each shape. Then make a chart of your results.

Did the same number of insects land on each shape? If they did, this would mean that it was just the colour that attracted them.

Do the experiment again. This time cut a flower shape out of red card. Put this alongside the yellow flower shape. Now watch and see if more insects visit your red or yellow flower shape.

▲ *This butterfly has landed on a buttercup.*

▼ *Draw bar charts to show the results of your experiments.*

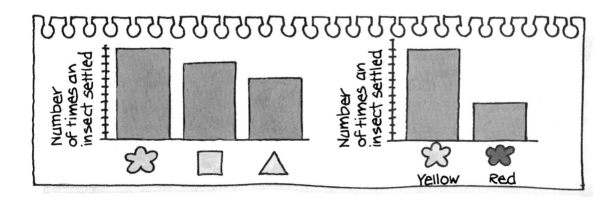

Mini beasts

Lots of mini beasts such as spiders, insects and woodlice are found on wasteland. There are many places where they can live and hide. Wasteland is often untidy, but makes a good home for creatures to live in. People, on the other hand, like their surroundings to be neat and tidy.

School fields and garden lawns are mown short, weeds are cleared and any litter collected up.

Find out if wasteland is a better for mini beasts than your school field. You can find out by setting up five **pitfall traps** on some wasteland.

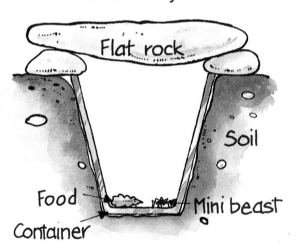

◀ *This is how to set up the pitfall trap to catch mini beasts.*

▼ *Three insects you may find in your pitfall trap.*

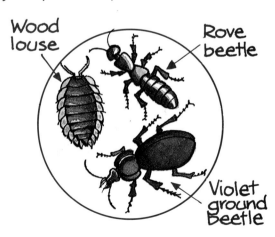

Warning: Don't forget to ask permission first before you dig any holes.

Set up another five traps on your school field or lawn at home. Leave the traps overnight, as night time is when mini beasts are most active. The mini beasts will fall into the traps and you can look at them in the morning.

The next day, empty the traps from the wasteland on to a white tray. Quickly count the mini beasts before you let them go. Do the same with the traps from the school field or lawn. Are there more mini beasts on your wasteland area than on mown grass?

Can you think of any ways that we make lawns and playing fields better places for mini beasts to live?

▲ *These mini beasts were caught on wasteland.*

▶ *These mini beasts were caught on a garden lawn.*

Be a predator

▲ *The caterpillar model looks like a twig.*

▲ *Someone has made a butterfly that looks like leaves.*

Animals that are hunted by **predators** are called **prey**. They are often **camouflaged**. This makes them difficult to see because they blend with their surroundings. Green caterpillars blend in with leaves, brown moths blend in with the trunks of trees. This helps them to hide from predators.

You can have fun playing the predator and prey game. First each person in the class should make the shape of a small animal out of cardboard and cut it out. The animal should be coloured so that it blends in with the place where it is commonly found.

When you have finished, collect the cards up.

The class is divided into two teams. One team will put the animals out on the in the school grounds where they are difficult to see. The other team can now play at being predators and hunt for the animal cards. See how many they find in 5 minutes.

After this everyone should collect the remaining animal cards. It is now the turn of the second team to put the animal cards outside. The first team hunts for the animal cards for 5 minutes.

Which team found the most animals in 5 minutes? Which team were the best predators? You could continue the game by making another set of animals. Make the camouflage even better so they are even more difficult for the other team to find.

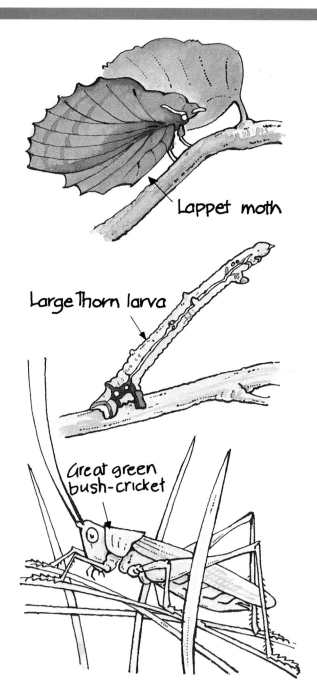

Lappet moth

Large Thorn larva

Great green bush-cricket

These animals have very good camouflage.

Nature trail

You have seen that wasteland is a very good habitat for wildlife. It would be fun to tell your friends about what animals and plants you have found in your piece of wasteland. You could also help to turn it into a mini **nature reserve**.

Plan a nature trail across the wasteland area. Decide how you want people to walk round it and what you would like them to see. Draw some arrows on sticks to show the way. Perhaps your visitors could investigate the following habitats:

1. Trees or bushes
2. A bath pond
3. A rotten log
4. Walls, concrete or loose bricks
5. Pathways

You could make some cards telling your visitors what plants and animals they might find in the habitats that you have suggested.

To show you value your piece of wasteland, you could show how you can improve it for wildlife. You could make a pond for water plants and animals to live in, sow some wildflower seeds or put in some rotten logs for insects like beetles to make their homes. Nest-boxes and bird-tables will encourage birds to live in your wasteland.

A wasteland nature trail.

GLOSSARY

Barren Describes a place where plants or flowers cannot grow.

Camouflaged The colours and patterns of an animal that makes it difficult to see.

Dispersed Spread about.

Environment The surroundings.

Habitat A natural place where plants and animals live.

Microscopic Something that is too small to be seen by the eye alone.

Mucus A slimy liquid produced by an animal.

Nature reserve A safe and natural area set up by humans for animals and plants to live in.

Nectar Liquid made by flowers which attracts insects.

Pitfall trap A jar buried in the soil with stones around the top.

Plantains Types of plants with broad leaves and small greenish flowers.

Potting compost Special soil for growing plants in.

Predators Animals that kill and eat other animals.

Prey Animals that are killed and eaten by other animals.

Tap root The main part of the plant that holds it in the ground.

Turf The surface layer of grass.

BOOKS TO READ

Bellamy, D. **Bellamy's Backyard Safari** (BBC, 1981)

Feltwell, J. **Discovering Doorstep Wildlife** (Hamlyn, 1985)

Taylor, N. **Mini Pets** (Wayland, 1992)

Shipp, D. **Spotter's Guide to Town and Country Wildlife** (Usborne, 1981)

Wilson, R. **The Urban Dweller's Wildlife Companion** (Blandford, 1983)

NOTES

This book involves learning about ecology through practical activities suitable for an area of waste ground. It is recommended that the activities for children should only be carried out under the supervision of a teacher.

p4-5 Bare land is invaded very quickly by certain types of plants, often these are species of weed. Invading plants modify the habitat making it suitable for other species to invade. The climax vegetation for most of Britain is different types of woodland.

p6-7 Flat plants such as daisies and plantains are resistant to trampling and will survive on trampled paths. The plants do not grow among taller vegetation because they cannot compete with the taller plants for light.

p8-9 Daisies take between 1 and 1½ hours to close after darkness.

p10-11 Seeds will germinate more rapidly in a warm humid atmosphere than a cool one. There will be condensation on the underside of the plastic. The covering has not only provided warmer conditions, but has prevented moisture loss from the soil.

p12-13 Certain types of litter, such as glass, may take thousands of years to rot away. The survey should show that there is more paper litter near the road as this is frequently dropped by passers-by. Paper would also have rotted away further from the road.

p14-15 The morning sun warms up the butterflies' wings for flight, and they are more likely to fly when the sun is out.

p16-17 Poppies are able to grow on bare and disturbed land because there are few plants to compete with.

p18-19 Species of weeds grow very quickly from seed to maturity, sometimes within a few months. They flower and set seed in a very short time. These strategies are ideal for types of plants that pioneer the invasion of waste or bare land.

p20-21 Snails roam quite long distances during the night. They will return to a good hiding place if there is one available.
In a snail maze, snails will avoid going over sandpaper if they can, by taking avoiding action. The silver trail of mucus is a method by which the snail can smooth out rough surfaces as it moves along. This investigation is more fun if it is turned into a snail race.

p22-3 It is the colour yellow and not the flower shape that attracts insects. Yellow is usually more attractive than red. The most common visitor to the cards will probably be hoverflies.

p24-5 Areas that are left unattended by people usually have more species of animals than mown grassland, such as the school playing field. Therefore there should be a larger catch of animals in the wasteland pitfall trap.

p26-7 Make sure the children do not hide their animal cards under things so they cannot be seen. It should be just the camouflage that makes the animals difficult to see. For safety, this activity is best carried out in the school grounds.

p28-9 To make a nature reserve in a wasteland area try and establish different varieties of plants that flower at different times and provide food and shelter for wildlife. Do not dig up wild plants but buy packet seeds of flowers to sow. Weeds and wild grasses provide food and hiding places for caterpillars and small mammals. Old logs attract homes for animals and insects. Make sure that if you adopt a piece of land that the owner is contacted first as permission will be required.

INDEX